IMAGES
of England

AROUND
UTTOXETER

High Street, Uttoxeter, 1914 (McCann). Alfred McCann photographed this solid-tyred Daimler bus from a window above his shop. In the background are the bay-windowed offices of Bunting's Brewery, built on the site of the old Cock Inn and demolished in the 1960s when the Maltings Shopping Precinct was built.

IMAGES
of England

AROUND
UTTOXETER

Compiled by
Roy Lewis

TEMPUS

First published 1999
Copyright © Roy Lewis, 1999

Tempus Publishing Limited
The Mill, Brimscombe Port,
Stroud, Gloucestershire, GL5 2QG

ISBN 0 7524 1513 1

Typesetting and origination by
Tempus Publishing Limited
Printed in Great Britain by
Midway Clark Printing, Wiltshire

For Jonwyn, Anita and Steven

Front Cover: High Street, Uttoxeter, 1926.

Bamford's Carnival lorry, late 1920s. This decorated lorry, with its display of agricultural machinery, was photographed in the Leighton Ironworks yard before taking part in the Uttoxeter Carnival procession.

Contents

Acknowledgements

To all who have written about Uttoxeter and district in the past, to librarians, archivists, museum curators, local historians, postcard collectors, and all who have generously shared their knowledge with me, I acknowledge my debt and gratitude. They have made the writing of this book a journey of discovery and pleasure. I hope readers will share this with me.

The following have given permission for photographs and postcards in their collections to be copied and reproduced. Numbers refer to pages and A and B to upper and lower illustrations respectively.

Staffordshire Arts and Museum Service: 2, 27A, 37B, 51A, 51B, 53B, 56B, 64B, 65A, 68B, 69, 71B, 73A, 80B, 91A, 93A, 98A, 99, 104A, 108A, 108B, 109B, 110A, 110B, 111A, 111B, 112A, 112B, 114, 115A, 117A, 117B, 118B, 123A, 123B, 124A.

Staffordshire Education Committee Quality Learning Services Support Unit: 10B, 13A, 13B, 16A, 16B, 17A, 17B, 19B, 23, 27B, 35B, 43A, 43B, 61B, 96B, 100, 102A, 102B, 105A, 106B, 113, 116A, 121A, 121B, 205A, 125A.

Uttoxeter Town Council and Heritage Centre: 9.

Uttoxeter Racecourse Leisure & Development Co. Ltd: 20B, 21.

J.C. Bamford Excavators Ltd: 119, 120A, 120B.

Russell Heath: 4, 33, 44, 101A, 103B, 107B.

Len Hopkins: 110B.

Basil Jeuda: 60B, 127A.

Randle Knight: 81.

Mrs Ivy Shore: 36, 45B, 46, 47, 72B, 73B, 93B, 103A, 115B, 128A.

Edward Talbot and Foxline Publishing Co.: 77A.

All other illustrations are reproduced from the Lewis family collection.

Introduction

Over 200 photographs and postcards showing people, places and events in and around Uttoxeter are reproduced in this book. Most are the work of professional local photographers. Their names, where they can be identified, or those of the postcard publishers are given in brackets after the title of each picture, to acknowledge their contribution to our knowledge of the town and its neighbourhood in years gone by.

By the 1850s photography had become more than a chemical curiosity. Glass plates with pre-treated surfaces were available and cameras were becoming less cumbersome. Early photographers were self-taught. Those who set up in business needed a dark workroom and a conservatory-style annexe with good light. These portraits and outdoor views were often small (60 x 90mm) and mounted on heavy card with the photographer's advertisement on the back.

Only a limited amount of work existed in a small town, so that photography was usually combined with another business. In the Uttoxeter area the first professional photographer was Thomas Bacon Allport, a local man whose studio and shoemaking business were both in the Market Place. His portraits of Uttoxeter citizens have survived until the modern day from the early 1860s to the late 1880s.

Another early photographer was Edward McCann. He had been born in Hereford in the 1820s and, after a military career in India, settled in Uttoxeter around 1860. He became Sergeant Major in the local Yeomanry Cavalry (the Territorial Army of the day) and was assistant overseer, responsible for collecting poor rates in the town. He bought a house on the west side of High Street and there his youngest son, Alfred, was born in 1865. In 1870 he began taking photographic portraits on the premises and by 1880 had also converted the front of the house into a tobacconist's shop. Alfred helped in the shop and was taught photography. In 1884, at the age of nineteen, Alfred took over both businesses, although his widowed father continued to live on the premises.

Other photographers set up in Uttoxeter later in the nineteenth century. R.J. Kelly, a long established printer and stationer with premises in the Market Place, was taking portraits from about 1890 until he sold the business a few years later. John Lamb, a newcomer to the town, opened a studio in Carter Street in 1895 but failed to make a living and moved to Cannock before 1900. George Elly also opened a studio in 1895 in Mount Pleasant. In the early 1900s he moved to Bridge Street where he opened a cycle shop, supplemented his income by helping to collect income tax and let his photographic business wither, although he was still advertising it in 1911.

Alfred McCann alone survived, by a mixture of business acumen and a reputation for putting sitters at their ease. In about 1900 he furnished a new studio with the latest photographic equipment and also opened a photographic shop at 27 High Street, adjoining the tobacconist's opened by his father. He advertised, 'Portraits in latest styles, wedding and other groups at moderate charges, pictures framed by machinery.'

His only competition came from Andrew Glover, a member of the Professional Photographers Association with a successful studio in Alfreton, who opened a branch studio at the corner of High Street and Smithfield Road in May 1909; 'High Class Real Photographs at Popular Prices' were promised. The studio closed soon after 1914, probably because the manager had been called up to fight in the war.

After the First World War, Alfred McCann was the only professional photographer in Uttoxeter. He died in 1943 and the business was then carried on by his son, Gerald, who specialized in photographing pedigree farm animals, until he retired in 1966. The building was sold in 1968 and is now a travel agency. Many of the McCann negatives are preserved in the County Museum at Shugborough.

Other photographers who should be noted include Revd Charles Frederick Lowry Barnwell, the long-serving vicar of Stramshall from 1879 to 1934, who produced a number of local views in the 1890s, and S.A. Johnson, who photographed people and events in Rocester from the early 1920s to the 1940s.

Picture postcards began to appear in Britain in 1894 but their use and availability spread very slowly until the early 1900s, after which they became immensely popular. The first cards of the Uttoxeter area were two views of Denstone College printed in 1898 by Louis Wilding, the Shrewsbury printer, whose son had been a pupil at the College. These had a limited sale within the College.

Surprisingly, the first local view postcards on general sale, came, not from Alfred McCann, but from a Londoner, E. Wrench, at the beginning of 1902. These were instantly popular and further cards were published later that year, including ones of Rocester and Marchington. Alfred McCann was quick to see the commercial possibilities and published his own series of cards printed in Germany early in 1903. Later that year, he followed these with photographic view cards, which he developed himself on pre-printed postcard backs. Soon he extended these to include cards of local events, and by 1909 he advertised 'over 600 views of Uttoxeter and district, a very fine collection, continually being added to.' He continued to produce photographic postcards until the late 1930s.

National publishers were soon printing cards of the district. Local shopkeepers could choose from series of cards produced by Frederick Hartmann or Raphael Tuck & Sons of London, Valentine & Sons of Dundee, William Shaw of Burslem and others. All of these used negatives from local photographers like McCann. Other photographers took pictures of the area for their own series of postcards. These included R. & R. Bull of Ashbourne (1905), W.H. Hall of Widnes (1907), Andrew Glover of Uttoxeter (1909-10) and the Doncaster Rotophoto Company (1921). Some shopkeepers commissioned their own series of cards, among them W.H. Smith & Son, who had a bookstall at Uttoxeter station and later a shop in the Market Place. Between 1920 and 1932 the Radermacher Aldous Publishing Co. of London also produced series of cards for Francis and Edward Harper, and Annie Kelly, all from Uttoxeter, and Phyllis Stanier from Leigh.

Since 1960 the number and variety of local views on postcards has steadily diminished. Today they only show a limited range of views that are most likely to appeal to visitors. Nevertheless they are still a valuable record of the changing face of Uttoxeter and the villages nearby.

Dates assigned to many of the postcards and photographs reproduced in this book are best-guesses based on a study of the pictures themselves and, for postcards, of the different formats used by photographers and publishers, and on postmark dates if the postcard has been postally used.

One
A Tour of Uttoxeter

Circus parade, Uttoxeter, early 1900s. When a travelling circus came to town, a parade of animals, performers and eye-catching set pieces, like the one in this picture, passed through the town centre to advertise its arrival and attract custom. This parade, seen passing along High Street, is certainly attracting attention.

Market day, Uttoxeter, 1903 (McCann). The market place has been the heart of Uttoxeter since the town was granted a weekly Wednesday market in the thirteenth century. This postcard shows china, brought to market in wicker baskets, laid out 'on the stones'. Farmers' wives came to market on carriers' wagons with large baskets of eggs and butter for sale. Once their produce was sold, they would do their weekly shopping before returning home.

Market day, Uttoxeter, 1912. By this time the use of market stalls was almost universal. In the centre of this photograph Andrew Dwyer of Rocester, draper, grocer and dealer, is unloading goods for his market stall from his horse-drawn van. On the left, behind the stalls, is the shop of W.H. Hearson, artistic printer, commercial and fancy stationer, bookseller, bookbinder, postcard publisher and dealer in toys, artists' materials and fancy goods.

The Market Place, Uttoxeter, 1909 (Glover). At this time the shops on this side of the Market Place were, from right to left: Edward Wilks, draper; Anthony Bradley, outfitter; Pakeman, grocer; Wyles Bros, shoes; The Vine, with its long sign 'Burton Brewery Co. – Celebrated Ales and Stouts'; George Stewart, butcher; and Orme & Sons, linen drapers. Pakeman's shop was rebuilt in 1910 and, soon afterwards, The Vine was also rebuilt as a mock Tudor black and white building, now occupied by The Leek United Building Society.

The Market Place, Uttoxeter, 1910 (Glover). This view shows the west end of the Market Place with The Old Talbot Inn, which sold Peter Walker's Burton-on-Trent brewed ale and beer, in the centre. The curious pile in the centre of the Market Place appears to have wheels and may be a cart with its load piled around it.

HOSPITAL SATURDAY, UTTOXETER ©

The Market Place on Hospital Saturday, 1910 (Glover). Every year on Hospital Saturday local inhabitants donated flowers to be sold for hospital funds. A stall was set up outside the Town Hall and volunteers with baskets and collecting boxes sold flowers on the streets. On the left can be seen the ornate three-light lamps outside Orme & Sons' shop. A little to the right is the scaffolding where Pakeman's shop is being rebuilt in the black and white Tudor style popular in the town during this period.

George Orme & Sons, Uttoxeter, 1907. George Orme opened a linen draper's shop in the late 1870s on the site of the shop seen above. By the mid 1890s this shop, selling ladies fashions as well as linen, was complemented by a gentlemen's tailor and outfitting shop in High Street. Later still, a furnishing department and a furniture removal service were added. This advertisement appeared in *A Handy Guide to Uttoxeter* priced twopence.

George Orme & Sons, 1911. The photographs on this page were both taken to advertise Ormes' shops. This one shows a range of ladies blouses, gloves and other wear displayed on the ground floor of London House, 9 Market Place (see opposite page).

George Orme & Sons, 1911. This is the interior of 5 Market Place, Orme and Sons' furniture department, with upholstered chairs, tables, bureaux, washstands with large basins and jugs, and many other items on display. Wooden chairs are hung from rails around the walls.

The Market Place, Uttoxeter, 1905 (Trent Bridge Publishing Co.). The black and white Tudor-style building on the right was divided in two. The right half was Crompton and Evans Union Bank in 1905. Later it became the Derby Old Bank, and later still the National Westminster bank (which rebuilt the premises). The other half was a shop belonging to John Furbank, a draper, costumier and silk mercer. After inheriting his mother's millinery shop in Balance Street, Furbank moved to these premises in about 1900 advertising 'smart dressmaking and stylish millinery'.

High Street from the Market Place, 1905 (R. & R. Bull). On the left are the premises of J. Phillips and Son, a family firm of plumbers and glaziers established in 1836. Next door is The Old Talbot Inn, perhaps the oldest building in Uttoxeter, and said to date from 1527. It survived the disastrous fires that swept through the town in 1596 and 1672. The Inn takes its name from the talbot, or hound, which was the crest of the Talbots, Earls of Shrewsbury.

The Kiosk, Uttoxeter, 1920. A conduit to supply water from underground springs to the inhabitants of the town stood in the Market Place until 1852, when the Market Place was refurbished and this building put in its place. Today its fame rests with Samuel Johnson, the Lichfield writer and dictionary compiler. Samuel's father, Michael Johnson, a dealer in old books, had a stall in Uttoxeter Market. One day, when he was unwell, he asked his son to stand in for him. Samuel refused. A number of years later Samuel returned to the town and stood bareheaded in the rain on the site of his father's stall in humble penance for his refusal. The incident is recorded by a bas-relief on one side of the Kiosk.

John Cope, butcher, 1911. The Cope family have owned a butcher's shop in Uttoxeter from the 1890s to the present day. This photograph shows John Cope and his assistants outside the shop at 1 Market Place. The display of meat hung unhygienically, by today's standards, from the outside rails was a normal sight at this time. The photographs on this page and the next one are taken from advertisements.

Albert Edward Carter, saddler, 1911. In the 1840s William Carter was making and selling saddles in Sheep Market and twenty years later his son had a shop in the Market Place. In about 1880 he also became a jobmaster hiring out traps, gigs and horses from the Church Street yard shown in this photograph. By 1911 both businesses were run by Albert Edward Carter. When they were separated in the 1920s, the jobmaster's yard became one of the town's first garages.

G. & A. Harris, ironmongers, 1911. George and Alfred Harris, general and furnishing ironmongers, implement agents and dealers in glass and china, opened their shop at 20 Market Place in about 1905. Their window and pavement displays show the range of their stock. On the first floor, three milk churns almost hide a sign saying that petrol was sold there.

Brewster & Co., tailors and outfitters, 1911. John Henry Brewster, tailor and outfitter, opened a shop in Carter Street at the beginning of this century and moved to 49 Market Place sometime before 1908. The advertisement accompanying this picture reads, 'We can suit you. We are now showing our NEW SEASON'S CLOTHES, including some lovely effects in the fashionable colours, BROWN AND GREEN. Men's suits from 25 to 75 shillings, to measure. We can suit your figure. We can suit your purse.'

Bridge Street, Uttoxeter, 1909 (W.H. Smith & Son). Bridge Street provides the route to the railway station and in 1909 residents complained that carts were being driven recklessly along it to deliver churns of milk in time to catch the milk train. During wakes week in September a pleasure fair, set up at the end of the street, caused more annoyance. One of the few shops was No. 50 where Thomas Carter sold gramophones, neophones and phonographs, supplied records (disc and cylinder) and charged accumulators.

Uttoxeter from the railway bridge, 1921 (Doncaster Rotophoto Co.). If you stand on the railway bridge today you will see that the view has hardly changed since this picture was taken. Trees still overhang the road, the pattern of roofs is unchanged and the spire of the parish church can still be seen in the distance – only the distant chimneys of Buntings Brewery have gone.

Uttoxeter railway station, 1909 (W.H. Smith & Son). The main London to Buxton railway line bypassed Uttoxeter. Main line trains had to stop at East Junction on that line and reverse into the platform shown here. In 1905 one of these trains ran down Sam Riley, a well known one-legged inhabitant, who was crossing to the other platform across the line instead of using the covered bridge seen in the distance. The Churnet Valley line used another platform further to the right.

The London milk train, 1910. Every evening farmers brought their milk to Uttoxeter station by pony and trap or cart in time to be loaded onto the milk train for London. Milk churns carrying seventeen gallons are being loaded onto the train at the platform which can be seen in the picture above. Not until 1933 was a collection service organized to bring milk from the farms.

Uttoxeter Steeplechase, first meeting, 1907 (McCann). Early in 1907 a company with a capital of £6,000 was formed to build a racecourse at Uttoxeter. The promoters hoped that it would attract more support than the course at Keele that had been forced to close. A site near the station was secured and early in April it was reported, 'The ground has been levelled and the North Staffordshire Railway has put in a siding. A grandstand is to be erected in time for races in early May.'

Uttoxeter racecourse, 1989. This picture shows the track at the racecourse after it was widened and re-drained. Since then over £5 million has been spent improving the facilities while sponsorship has raised prize money to more than £700,000, attracting top trainers and the best horses. The race shown here was sponsored by Trent Bathrooms of Hanley.

The Prince Edward Grandstand, October 1994. At Uttoxeter racecourse a new grandstand with a large betting hall, good catering facilities, and eighteen private viewing boxes was opened by HRH Prince Edward and named in his honour. The Prince is seen here with Stanley W. Clarke, CBE, chairman of the Racecourse Leisure and Development Company.

Church Street, Uttoxeter, 1914. On the left is the residence of the Medical Officer of Health to the UDC and next to it, set back out of sight, the vicarage. The covered cart in the street carries the initials DCS (Derby Cooperative Society). The Society opened a shop in Carter Street in June 1907, marking the occasion with a public tea in the Town Hall followed by musical entertainment.

Bridge Street, Uttoxeter, 1909 (W.H. Smith & Son). The three-storey brick building on the right, with the very large dog outside, is the White Horse Inn, licensee, Henry Stokes. Beyond it is George Woolley's saddlery shop with its projecting window and sign advertising 'Everett's polishes by Appointment to His Majesty the King'.

Mary Howitt's house, Balance Street, Uttoxeter, 1910 (McCann). Samuel Botham, a Quaker who is buried in the small churchyard behind the Friends' Meeting House in Uttoxeter, lived in this house at the beginning of the nineteenth century. His daughter, Mary, grew up here and married William Howitt, a young poet. As Mary Howitt, she wrote many popular children's books and translated Hans Christian Anderson's works into English. She collaborated with her husband in *The Forest Minstrel*, a book of poetry, and a variety of other bestselling books. In later life they lived abroad. Mary died in Rome in 1888. In 1881 Francis Redfern wrote that at the back of Mary's house 'a flower garden sloped towards the valley. The part next to the road has recently been altered and now belongs to H. Hawthorn, surgeon.'

Balance Street, Uttoxeter, 1909 (W.H. Smith & Son). On the right of the picture is the eighteenth-century Vernon House, for many years the home of the Vernon family, who had a cork cutting business in the town. They also dealt in calves' maw skins, used to curdle milk for making cheese. In 1895 the building was restored and converted into flats by the East Staffordshire Heritage Trust. On the left is the police station and buildings demolished when Uttoxeter Nursing Home was extended.

Balance Street, Uttoxeter, 1910 (McCann). This picture shows the same street from the opposite direction to the view above. The prominent two-storey bay window on the right still survives, but without its flagpole. On the opposite side of the road is the Roman Catholic church, as it was before it was altered in 1914. In the foreground are the premises of Walter Colbourne, a painter and decorator who lived next to The Greyhound Inn. Both of these buildings have now been pulled down.

Balance Street, Uttoxeter, 1909 (Glover). The 'G' identifies this as one of the postcards published by Andrew Glover at his studio on the corner of High Street and Smithfield Road. Leighton Terrace, built about 1750, is on the right and Pinfold Street runs by the side of the low double-gabled building beyond it. Notice the brick and cobble pavement at the side of the road.

Balance Street, looking west, Uttoxeter, 1905 (R. & R. Bull). On the left, with its tall gable, is Leighton House, now occupied by Synopsis Design. The front of the low building beyond it, now the veterinary surgery of Cooper and Partners, has been appropriately decorated with stone horses' heads. In the distance is Mary Howitt's house (see p. 23).

The White Hart Hotel, 1914. In the early nineteenth century this was the town's main coaching inn. It was a place for coaches travelling between London and Liverpool, Manchester and Birmingham, and Newcastle-under-Lyme and Derby to stop and change horses. By 1914 the hotel hired out wagonettes, dog carts, and a handsome wedding carriage with a matching pair of greys. Beyond the porch the round Michelin sign of the hotel's motor garage can be seen.

Carter Street, Uttoxeter, 1909 (W.H. Smith & Son). On the right are shops belonging to J.H. Greenwood, a dealer in woollen goods, and Samuel Durose a supplier of 'refreshments and tobacco'. Beyond The White Hart and the half-timbered building that is now the Heritage Centre was the clothing shop of Richard Shaw. This shop was well known for the rhyming ditties that the owner put in his window to draw attention to his stock.

Carter Street, Uttoxeter, *c.* 1890 (Revd Barnwell). This row of old half-timbered, thatched houses were built on stone foundations and could be found on the corner of Carter Street and a very narrow Stone Road. A sign to Sandon, Stafford and Stone is fastened to the end wall in the shape of a hand. Today the site is occupied by the maisonettes of Jubilee Court.

Laythropp's Almhouses, 1910. In 1700 William Laythropp, son of Humphrey Laythropp of Crakemarsh, left four houses in Carter Street to be used as almshouses for poor widows. A small income from other rents went to repair the houses and, if possible, provide fuel for the widows. The houses were rebuilt in 1848 by Thomas Fradgley at a cost of £300.

Hockley Road, Uttoxeter, 1906 (Frederick Hartmann). The houses in this picture were almost the last ones on the road to Stafford. On the left, they backed onto gardens and fields, which have now become part of the factory operated by JCB SCM Ltd. Today the factory entrance is just beyond the houses. On the right is a row of villas built a few years before this postcard was published.

'Brooklyn', 1915 (McCann). It was around this time that a man named Ralph and his wife moved into 'Brooklyn', one of the villas in the picture above. 'This will give you an idea of our garden', he wrote on this postcard to his mother, 'but you must come and see for yourself.' The woman in the picture is Ralph's wife, Kate, but the identity of Ralph remains unknown.

Hockley level crossing, 1907 (W. Shaw). In the foreground Picknall Brook flows under the bridge. On the far side of the Brook the railway lines to Stafford and Stone cross the road at Hockley level crossing. The crossing keeper's house is next to the gates. In 1907 these were wrecked when the horses pulling the mail coach from Stafford took fright at Blount's Green and bolted down the hill, straight into the closed gates.

The cemetery, Uttoxeter, 1909 (W.H. Smith & Son). The cemetery on Hockley Road was established in 1861. At the same time a lodge for the cemetery keeper and a mortuary chapel, designed by Wilson of Derby in Gothic style, were also built. In recent years the spire of the chapel became unsafe and had to be pulled down.

The old sexton in Uttoxeter cemetery, 1907 (W.H. Hall). When the cemetery was opened in 1861 Benjamin Yates was appointed as the first cemetery keeper and sexton. He lived in the lodge and carried out his duties until he died in November 1907, aged 82. In this postcard he has his hand on the headstone of John Sharratt of Uttoxeter, who died in 1887 aged 78, and Betty his wife, who died the following year.

High Street, Uttoxeter, 1904 (W. Shaw). On the right are the shops of Albert Carter, a saddler, and Arthur Bayley, a grocer and confectioner. On the opposite side of the road another grocery shop advertises Camp coffee and Rowntrees cocoa in its window while a delivery of Dermo flour has been left on the pavement. Carter Street branches off on the left and, in the distance, are road works which can be seen more clearly on p. 36.

The White Hart omnibus, 1907 (W.H. Hall). The omnibus from The White Hart conveyed those staying at the Hotel to and from the railway station. The charge was sixpence per person and this included baggage. Unusually, it is seen here in High Street, passing Huggins & Chambers ironmongers shop with its projecting 'Petrol' sign. In November 1921 the shop and its petrol store caught fire; flames rose to sixty feet and the shop was burnt out.

High Street, Uttoxeter, 1906 (W. Shaw). The two postcards on this page show almost identical scenes twenty years apart. In the right foreground is Bell & Dams, a family clockmaking and jewellery business started by Edward Bell in the eighteenth century. Next door is the gentlemen's tailoring department or 'Grand Clothing Hall' of Orme & Sons with its large first floor display windows. Huggins & Chambers shop can be seen on the left.

High Street, Uttoxeter, 1926 (W. Shaw). By this time the new building for William Deacon's Bank has replaced Bell & Dams shop and the first floor windows of Orme & Sons have been altered. After the fire in 1921, the site of Huggins & Chambers shop was bought by Barclays Bank who built the black and white Tudor-style building seen here. The upper floors of the bank building were occupied by Charles Elkes, whose café and bakery were next door.

George Hankinson, late Johnson, 1903 (McCann). In 1780 Thomas Woolrich established his business as a chemist and druggist in High Street, Uttoxeter. A century later it was Woolrich & Johnson and by the time this picture was taken it had been changed to Hankinson late Johnson. As well as the chemist's shop, which also sold photographic materials, the business had an agricultural department. This manufactured and sold medicines for horses and cattle based on remedies handed down with the business since 1780. These were used over a wide area. Hankinson late Johnson also had a department supplying seeds for fields and gardens. The shop was sold to Boots the Chemist in 1921 but the agricultural department continued to manufacture medicines from premises in Church Street.

The Cross Keys, 1905. This High Street building has '1697, Edward Hadley, builder', carved on it. It is one of the few seventeenth-century buildings in the area built using brick, instead of the more popular timber framing. Before the Town Hall was built, public meetings and magistrates' courts were held here. The premises are now occupied by Bagshaws, the estate agents and auctioneers.

Blackwell Bros, 1906 (W. Shaw). In 1905, when the picture on the opposite page was published, the licensee of the Cross Keys was Charles Sampson, a Hampshire man. Sampson had spent many years as a missionary to the Eskimos before buying the *Forget-me-not*, a small ship in which he spent two years hunting seals in the Arctic. In 1903, he returned to England and became the licensee of the Cross Keys. Five years later, he and his wife took over the shoe business of Blackwell Bros, opposite the Cross Keys.

High Street, Uttoxeter, 1905. These shops with gable-end frontages are seventeenth-century timber-framed buildings with their fronts plastered over to hide the framing. Much of their original appearance was restored in 1988. It is worth noting the fine display of local postcards outside the stationery shop next to Harold Chitty's florist's shop.

Uttoxeter entrenched, 1904 (McCann). In this picture High Street is being dug up so that a 'complete sewage plan on the bacterial filter system' could be laid. This effort to improve the town's health was carried out by Messrs Wilcox and Railkes at a cost of £20,000 and was badly needed. The photograph was taken by Alfred McCann, whose shop with its projecting 'Tobacco' sign can be seen on the right. His photographic shop and studio were next door. Soon after the photograph was taken the upper part of McCann's shop was rebuilt with projecting bay windows and an additional storey. A new shop front with larger windows was put in at the same time. The premises are now occupied by the Lunn Poly holiday shop. On the opposite side of the road, shops are advertising that they are agents for 'Raglan' and 'Whitworth' bicycles.

High Street, Uttoxeter.

High Street, Uttoxeter, 1926 (W. Shaw). On the left is the Town Hall that opened in 1854 to provide a magistrates' court, a police station with cells and a room for local functions. The mock black and white building next to it, now replaced by Wilkinsons, was the Town Hall keeper's house. Many of the buildings opposite the Town Hall were pulled down when the Maltings Shopping Precinct was built.

Off to Alton Towers, 1930s (McCann). Lady Shrewsbury lived at Alton Towers until 1923. In the following year the house and its grounds were sold to a group of local businessmen. The new owners greatly improved the grounds and installed catering facilities for the increasingly large number of people who came to enjoy the gardens. In this photograph a convoy of coaches is passing along High Street on its way to the gardens.

High Street, Uttoxeter.

High Street, Uttoxeter, 1926 (W. Shaw). On the corner of Manor Road (the turning to the left in the foreground) is the Hope and Anchor public house. On the right of the street lamp, the house with the ornate gable was the home of the Revd Robert Hughes, the Congregational Minister.

HIGH STREET, UTTOXETER.

High Street, Uttoxeter, 1907 (W. Shaw). On the left are the wall and trees of the Manor House grounds. On the right is the Wellington Inn, licensed to Harriet Rollinson, with an arch providing a passage to a yard at the rear. On the far right are the premises of Mary Ward, a dealer in china. Today, Mary Ward's house has been pulled down to make a car park and part of the Manor House wall was demolished when the Elite Cinema was built.

The Manor House, Uttoxeter, 1913 (McCann). This is an old house with a varied history. A plaque on the wall informs the passer-by that Admiral Lord Gardner was born here in 1742. Three years later the Duke of Cumberland stayed here during his pursuit of Bonnie Prince Charlie. In the late nineteenth century Misses Marion and Dorothy Hawthorn opened the Manor House School for young ladies (see p. 45).

Manor Road, Uttoxeter, 1926 (W. Shaw). These were the first council houses built in Uttoxeter. The estate was planned in 1920 and the first tenants arrived in 1921, paying a rent of between 6s 6d and 9s per week. A competition to name the street was won by Mrs Hearson who suggested Manor Road because the land adjoined the Manor House. She asked that her two guineas prize should be used to buy a seat in the Recreation Ground.

Uttoxeter from the air, looking east, 1925 (McCann). This is one of the first aerial views of Uttoxeter, taken by Alfred McCann. In the middle distance is Bunting's Brewery with its tall chimney and in the foreground is Stone Road. Between them are the cattle market and the roofs of buildings in the High Street. On the left, houses in Manor Road have just been built but most of the area left of Smithfield Road is still fields and allotments.

New Street, Uttoxeter, 1907 (W.H. Hall). This is one of the pictures that W.H. Hall, a photographer from Widnes, took of Uttoxeter and Rocester and published as postcards. In 1907 the street was newly laid. Today it looks almost exactly the same except for television aerials and a few doors and windows that have been replaced.

40

The Wharf, Uttoxeter, 1906 (McCann). The Uttoxeter branch of the Caldon Canal had once terminated at the back of these houses. On the left is Cheadle Road and along it, just out of sight, 'The Limes' (now The Limes Hotel) which had been the canal wharfmaster's house. In the centre was Collis' bakery and confectioner's shop. A delivery boy with his basket is posed outside and a horse-drawn delivery van is parked between the houses.

The Wharf, Uttoxeter, 1950s. This is the same scene as the photograph above but from about fifty years later. On the left, The Union public house and nearby houses were demolished when Elkes' factory was expanded. An oak tree was planted in the centre of what came to be called Park Place to mark the coronation of George V in 1911 (see p. 105). Today the site is a roundabout for traffic. The shop that had belonged to Collis in 1906 was owned by J.J. Walker in the 1950s.

Alleyne's Grammar School, 1903 (McCann). In 1847 the house on the right was bought for the headmaster of Alleyne's Grammar School. Twelve years later the schoolroom on the left was built and the school moved to this site. The bell above the schoolroom was always rung five minutes before school commenced. In 1903 a laboratory some distance from the schoolroom was in use and the pupils built their own telephone to link it to the headmaster's desk in the schoolroom. A new laboratory next to the schoolroom was opened in 1904.

Dove Bank, Uttoxeter, 1908 (McCann). These houses stand just beyond the embankment that marks the line where the railway crossed Derby Road. The date when these houses were built can be fixed because when the sash windows of the house on the left were put in, the carpenter secured a better fit by using a page from a 1907 magazine. Notice the lack of traffic that allowed a man to walk home in the middle of the road.

Bradley Street, Uttoxeter, *c.* 1960. In the 1960s Bunting's maltings, which had been vacant for much of the time since the brewery had closed in the 1930s, was pulled down along with these houses on the south side of Bradley Street. The new bus station now occupies this site. This photograph was taken when most of the property was vacant and awaiting demolition.

View from the church tower, 1970s. This is the view looking north from the tower of the parish church towards Bradley Street, after the area had been redeveloped. The new bus station can be seen beyond the Maltings Shopping Precinct, Tesco, and the car park.

Accident on Dove Bank, Uttoxeter, 1929 (McCann). Early February of this year was cold with blizzards sweeping across the Midlands, temperatures remaining below zero all day and the roads being particularly treacherous. Early on the morning of Saturday 9 February, a six-wheeled lorry loaded with scrap iron was coming down Dove Bank when it skidded and crashed into the end of Mr James Harrison's house. This photograph shows the result. Incredibly no one was injured.

Uttoxeter Girls' High School, 1926 (W. Shaw). The Manor House School (see p. 39) was a private school for girls occupying The Hall on Dove Bank. In 1919 the school was taken over by the Staffordshire Education Committee and renamed Uttoxeter Girls' High School. A kindergarten attached to the school was housed in the grounds of Red Gables in the High Street. Red Gables also provided a small boarding establishment for about a dozen girls.

The gymnasium, Uttoxeter Girls' High School, 1928. The Hall building remained largely unaltered when it became a school. The kitchen in the basement was used to cook dinners for pupils and doubled as the domestic science room. Two rooms on the ground floor, separated by a movable partition, were used as the assembly hall, art room and gymnasium. The rooms on the upper floors were classrooms, a library and a music room.

Uttoxeter Girls' High School, 1931/2. In 1931 Miss W.M. Cooper succeeded Miss H. Woodhead as headmistress and is seen in the centre of the front row of this school photograph.

TUITION FEE: £3 10s. 0d. per term.

OPTIONAL SUBJECTS: Piano, £2 2s. 0d. per term.   Special Fees for Advanced Pupils.
Violin   -   -   -   £2 2s. 0d. ,, ,,
Dancing (in the winter terms)   £1 1s. 0d. ,, ,,
Elocution   -   -   -   £1 10s. 0d. ,, ,,

BOARDERS. Accommodation for a limited number of boarders is provided at Red Gables, High Street.
Fees (not including laundry), Termly Boarders—£17 0s. 0d. per term.
                                        Weekly   ,,   —£16 0s. 0d. ,,   ,,

DINNER HOUR. A two-course dinner is provided at the School. Tickets for this may be obtained at the School at the price of 1/- singly, or 10/6 per dozen.
Girls who bring their own dinner are required to have it in the dining room. Plates and glasses are provided, for which a charge of $\frac{1}{2}$d. per day is made.
No girl may have dinner elsewhere in the town except when accompanied by her parent or some other responsible person.

The other staff are, from left to right: Miss Scotter, Miss Price, -?-, -?-, Miss Beck, the Headmistress, Miss Walker, -?-, Miss Malvern, Miss Kirby, Miss Thomas, -?-. Extracts from the school prospectus at the time are reproduced below.

DRESS. Each pupil must have at school, a pair of slippers, a pair of rubber-soled gymnasium shoes, a pair of stockings and a blue cotton shoe bag.

All articles of clothing brought to School must be clearly marked with the owner's name.

Hair must be tied back with black or navy blue ribbon.

No jewellery, except brooches, may be worn at School.

No colours but navy blue and emerald green may be worn.

Each girl must have a navy blue gymnasium tunic with girdle for games and drill, and it is recommended that this should be worn daily.

Each girl must wear in summer a white straw hat (Panama or imitation) and in winter a navy blue cap, with the School hat band and badge. Navy blue coats must be worn. The wearing of the School tie is optional.

GAMES. Every girl, unless excused by Medical Certificate, is required to take part in the organised games of the School. Hockey and Netball are played in the Autumn and Spring Terms, Cricket and Tennis in the Summer Term.

Oldfields Hall, 1920 (McCann). Oldfields House was built in the late eighteenth century. In the nineteenth century it became Martha Bennett's school and then Charles Ford's home, before being bought by John Bamford of the Leighton Ironworks. After alterations to the building, he renamed it Oldfields Hall. Today it is part of Oldfields Hall Middle School.

Oldfields Cricket Club pavilion, 1906 (McCann). John Bamford was such a cricket enthusiast that he laid out a cricket ground, with the pavilion seen above, near his home. The facilities were of such a high quality that after a visit Dr W.G. Grace described it as 'one of the finest pavilions and best laid out grounds in the country'.

MCC/Australian XI v. Mr John Bamford's England XI, 1908 (McCann). John Bamford inaugurated an annual September Cricket Festival with a match between two teams of invited celebrities. This picture shows the 1908 festival match. John Bamford is seated in the middle of the front row of the MCC/Australian XI that includes such legendary names as Hobbs, Gunn, Hardstaff, Rhodes, Crawford, A.O. Jones and Blythe. Mr John Bamford's XI scored 180 and MCC/Australia 201 before rain interrupted the match.

Hockey at Uttoxeter, 1908/9 (McCann). Uttoxeter Ladies' hockey team can be seen playing a home match. During this period long skirts and blouses with ties were the normal dress for hockey players. The teams could be differentiated by the colour of their ties.

The Recreation Ground, Uttoxeter, 1926 (W. Shaw). In 1921 the Urban District Council set up a committee to provide a recreation ground. C.H. Elkes offered an eleven acre field sloping down to Picknall Brook and, in 1923, the council agreed to a threepenny rate to pay for its development. Plans for various sports facilities and a swimming pool were made, but when the Recreation Ground was opened in 1925 many of these were still waiting for funds to be raised.

The bathing pool, Uttoxeter, 1953 (Valentine & Sons). The Uttoxeter Amateur Swimming Club had changing rooms and a bathing place in the Dove where contests were held before 1900. Later these were abandoned for safety reasons. A new open air swimming pool in the Recreation Ground was opened in 1930. The rectangular concrete pool was filled from Picknall Brook and had simple changing rooms and a few lifebelts for safety.

The Lido, Uttoxeter, 1960s (McCann). The original pool was fed from Picknall Brook and later there were concerns expressed about the pollution of the water. A new open air pool was planned as part of a Lido with up-to-date water filtration, diving boards and better changing facilities. This photograph shows the pool nearing completion.

The paddling pool, 1960s (McCann). At the same time as the new open air swimming pool was being built, a paddling pool was constructed next to it. Workmen can be seen completing the sealing of the pool while, on the far left, other workmen can be seen applying turf to the surrounding area.

The third annual Uttoxeter Carnival, 1927 (McCann). In 1925 the first Uttoxeter Carnival was held to raise money for additional facilities at the Recreation Ground. The Carnival King (Mr B. Shaw) and Queen (Mr G. Hodgkins) were met at the railway station by a coach lent by Mrs Cavendish of Crakemarsh Hall, with attendants in scarlet coats and a court jester (Miss Edith Shaw). They were received by the 'Mayor' who gave them a large key to the town for the day. The Queen was also presented with a bouquet of carrots and onions. The King then knighted the 'Mayor' (Councillor H. Lowis) and invited him to join them in his coach. The procession of decorated vehicles, bands and pedestrians in costume toured the town, finishing at the racecourse for sports, morris dancing and gymnastics displays, and sideshows. The Women's Institute organized a baby show and there was a carnival dance at the Town Hall in the evening.

The Carnival Queen, 1934 (McCann). The 1933 carnival had raised little money and so the following year it was planned differently, with the money raised going to the Uttoxeter Nursing Association and hospitals in Stoke and Derby. The new carnival was centred round a local Carnival Queen chosen at a Town Hall dance. In June the procession was nearly a mile long and there were 'frolics until midnight'. The Queen, seen above, was Eva Rock of Carter Street with Kathleen Cockersole, Kathleen Jardine, Maud Tooth and Betsy Roberts as ladies-in-waiting.

The Dove Valley Players, 1930s (McCann). The Dove Valley Players were well known in the area during this period. The quartet were, from left to right: Nancy Reeves (accordion), Joy Lawrence (drums), Fred Jenkinson (violin) and Lena Stafford (piano). They are pictured here playing in the Haddon Room at Elkes café.

The Mikado, 1904 (McCann). The third production of the Uttoxeter Amateur Operatic Society was *The Mikado*. The conductor was Rawlinson Wood of Denstone College (middle of back row). Others taking part included: Mr H.P. Huggins (Mikado), Mr E. Laverton (Ko-Ko), Mr F. Godbehere (Pish-Tush), Mr A. Lasbrey (Nanki-Poo), Mr E. Wain (Pooh-Bah), Mrs Harry Ford (Yum-Yum), Miss Frances Nuttall (Pitti-Sing), Miss H. Luscombe (Peep Bo) and Mrs G. Rigby (Katisha).

Flooding of the Dove, 1903 (McCann). The autumn of 1903 was wet and led the *Staffordshire Advertiser* to report that there was 'the almost unexampled deluge of rain, the heaviest recorded for many years'. Many parts of Staffordshire had more than five inches of rain in October and this led to roads becoming flooded and riverside pastures being submerged. Late in October Alfred McCann took this view of Uttoxeter seen from the far side of the swollen Dove.

Two
Denstone and Rocester

Rocester Carnival, 1922. The annual carnival was Rocester's most popular attraction in the 1920s. In this photograph the Rocester Brass Band, preceded by a troupe of high-stepping girls and followed by the Union Friendly Society with its banner bearing the motto *Unity is Strength*, is seen passing Dwyer's shop in Ashbourne Road.

The Royal Oak, Denstone, 1912 (W. Shaw). This public house in Oak Road was demolished in 1965 and the new Denstone School is being built very close to this site. The last landlord was Mr Eardley whose daughter-in-law held ballet classes in a room over the stables in the 1940s. At the time this picture was taken the landlord was Jervis Green.

Denstone station, 1907 (McCann). The Churnet Valley line through Denstone opened in July 1849. To reduce expense, the line used the bed of the disused Uttoxeter Canal where possible. Denstone station was small and the platform in the foreground very low. When a train came to a halt there, a small set of steps was placed at the door of the first class carriage so that ladies could alight with decorum.

The Heywood Memorial, Denstone, 1934 (Scarratt). Sir Thomas Percival Heywood was the son of a Manchester banker. He bought Doveleys, just outside Denstone, and was a great benefactor to the village. He was largely responsible for the village becoming a separate parish and built the church, vicarage, and school there, as well as donating the site for Denstone College. In 1900 this red Hollington stone memorial was erected by villagers and friends in remembrance of Sir Thomas and his wife.

Denstone School, 1926-7. Denstone C of E School was built in 1866 by G.E. Street, the architect of the parish church, at the expense of Sir Thomas Heywood. In 1927 its eighty pupils were taught by Alfred Colley (headmaster), Miss Eleanor Woodrow and a Miss Salt, who was in charge of the infants. Each year rewards were given to encourage good attendance and these pupils had attended every day for at least a year.

Denstone College, 1928 (Aerophoto Co. Ltd). In the nineteenth century Canon Woodard founded a number of public schools to provide a Church of England education. One of these was Denstone College, where building began in 1868 on a site given by Sir Thomas Heywood. The original building was planned in the shape of an 'H'. The school opened in 1873 with 46 boys and by the 1920s had 300 pupils. The preparatory school buildings are in the foreground.

Denstone College, the Big Schoolroom, 1910 (McCann). The Big Schoolroom was 130 feet long with a portrait of the founder at the far end. There are masters' desks at each end so that more than one class could be taught. It is also interesting to note the desks with backless seats and the oil lamps overhead.

Denstone College, the swimming pool, 1910. As early as 1877 the College had an outdoor swimming pool, used by pupils in the summer term. This was later improved and a wooden diving platform added at one end. This photograph shows the end of a race watched by staff and pupils, some of whom are wearing the uniform of the College's Officer Training Corps.

Denstone College, the science laboratory, 1920 (Marshall, Keen & Co.). This postcard is one of a series showing the College in 1919/20. The master who sent this card on 26 March 1920 wrote, 'Two nurses are looking after forty-eight pupils who have mumps, and more cases keep coming every day.'

Rocester station, 1907 (W.H. Hall). The North Staffordshire Railway's Churnet Valley line to Leek and Macclesfield ran east of Stubwood, about half a mile from the centre of the village. A branch to Ashbourne curved away just out of sight on the left of this photograph. The junction was controlled by the signal box on the left. The station buildings are on the right and the crossing gates, where the line went over the road to Tean, can be seen in front of the buildings.

Rocester station, 1905 (McCann). The board advises passengers to change here for Ashbourne and Buxton. Signs for the Porters' Room and Gentlemen's First Class Waiting Room can be clearly seen and the sign for a similar Ladies' Waiting Room is half hidden in the shadow of the canopy over the platform. Note the milk churns awaiting collection.

The Railway Hotel, Rocester, 1911 (W. Shaw). The hotel was built in the 1850s soon after the Churnet Valley line was completed. In 1857 it became the meeting place of the Loyal Prince of Wales Lodge of Oddfellows, whose feast was held every June in a marquee pitched in the field opposite the hotel. At the time of this picture the landlord was Robert Jardine who had been there since the 1890s. The chimney on the right belongs to the Red Hill Bank brickworks (see p. 128).

Ashbourne Road level crossing, Rocester, mid 1960s. The line to Ashbourne and Buxton opened in 1852 and crossed the Ashbourne road at this point, just north of the present day Northfield Avenue. The line was closed to passengers in 1965 and these children posed on the gate around this date. Soon afterwards the line was taken up and the crossing dismantled.

Corn mill and Churnet bridge, Rocester, 1908 (W. Blake). This mill was driven by water from the Churnet. A head of water was built up by the weir and a short mill race near the building fed water to the wheel seen on the right. The building was originally a corn mill, but later ground potters' materials and then, with the water wheel removed, was converted into offices. In the early 1900s it was worked by Alfred Stanton and Thomas Bettany, who also owned stone quarries at Hollington, and dressed some of the stone alongside the mill.

High Street, Rocester, 1903 (McCann). This view of the junction of High Street and Ashbourne Road was one of the postcards that Alfred McCann had printed in German. On the far right is The Cross Keys and, on the opposite corner of Ashbourne Road, The Red Lion. The Union Friendly Society had its clubroom at The Red Lion and The Houldsworth Lodge of Oddfellows met at The Cross Keys (see p. 102). Only The Red Lion survives today.

High Street, Rocester, 1907 (W.H. Hall). The shop on the left with a clock over it belonged to George Slaney, who combined the business of hairdressing with selling jewellery. In the distance is the Primitive Methodist chapel (see p. 92). Slaney's shop was demolished in the 1960s.

Mill Lane, Rocester, 1907 (W.H. Hall). These two- and three-storied houses with outside shutters were built about 1800 for workers at the cotton mill. The downpipes stopped several feet above the ground so that, when it rained, water gushed across the pavement. The photographer carefully posed some of the children who lived in the houses and a sergeant on leave from the Royal Artillery with his wife or girlfriend, before he took the photograph.

Mill Lane, Rocester, 1907 (W.H. Hall). This view of Mill Lane seen from near its junction with Ashbourne Road is unrecognisable today. On the left is the smithy worked by William Brain, who brought his wife and family out of their home next door to pose for the photographer. Around them are horses waiting to be shod and farm machines sent for repair.

Ashbourne Road, Rocester, 1905 (McCann). On the left is the archway into the yard of The Red Lion and next to it is the busy shop of Andrew Dwyer, with its window advertisement for Bovril. Although Dwyer described himself as a grocer, his shop also sold shovels and other hardware. Signs on the wall advertise the fact that he was also an agent for John Smith, a dry cleaner, and stocked Royal Daylight lamp oil.

Rocester School, 1905 (McCann). The first school in Rocester was opened here in 1830 with a house for the master next to it. At first, teaching was on a monitorial system where the master taught eight monitors and they in turn taught the other fifty pupils in groups. The school was enlarged to take 220 pupils in 1880. In 1891 a school board was set up and a school rate levied on every household to pay for the school. At the time of this picture the headmaster was John Gandy and the girls' mistress was Agnes Slater.

Dove Lane, Rocester, 1903. John and Charles Lyons, owners of the cotton mill, built many of the houses in Dove Lane in the late 1870s for those who worked at the mill. The school on the right was built for infants in 1852. The original plans show that one end of the building was meant to be a newspaper reading room in the evenings.

Church Lane, Rocester, 1907 (W.H. Hall). This view is taken from near the vicarage, looking westward towards Ashbourne Road. In the distance, on the right, is the Post and Telegraph Office with a pole outside and a notice telling passers-by, 'You can telephone from here'. Beyond it is The Queen's Arms. Further in the distance the premises of Sheldon, a builder and wheelwright, can be seen on Ashbourne Road.

Barrow Hill, Rocester, 1907 (McCann). This house, built around 1780, was the home of the Dawsons, a family popular locally in the early twentieth century. In 1900, Captain Henry Dawson returned home from Bloemfontein having fought in the Boer War. He had been wounded and lost a leg after it was amputated. The villagers decorated the streets, took the horses out of the carriage sent to meet him, and drew him and the carriage from the station to Barrow Hill in a procession led by the Rocester Brass Band.

Rocester Carnival, 1921. These two pictures each show parts of the carnival procession in High Street. On the right a group of small children, their banner unfortunately illegible, are followed by the Rocester Brass Band. Below, a patriotic float with girls representing England, Scotland and Wales is followed by various pedestrians and riders in fancy dress.

Rocester Carnival, 1921. This cart has been decorated with a harvest scene, even the horse has his mane tied with ribbons and his harness decorated with brasses. The child in a pierrot costume seems rather out of place. The photograph was taken near the Churnet Bridge.

Rocester Silver Jubilee Jazz Band, 1935 (McCann). In 1935 King George V and Queen Mary had reigned for 25 years. Their Silver Jubilee was celebrated both nationally and in every town and village. This Rocester marching band took its title from the occasion. They entered the Uttoxeter Carnival and were photographed giving their display in front of the grandstand crowd at the racecourse.

Three
Other Villages in the Neighbourhood

Golf at Bramshall, 1920s (McCann). William Armett laid out a golf course on his land at Bramshall in the early 1920s and an elaborate pavilion was built there by Mr Hammersley. In this photograph Charles Bunting is driving off the first tee during a competition held around this time. After Mr Armett died, the popularity of the course declined and it closed during the Second World War.

Crakemarsh Hall, 1912. The Hall with its distinctive two-storey polygonal bays was built in the early 1800s on the site of a much older house. A 'sumptuous seventeenth-century staircase', removed from another house, was incorporated into the building. The house passed from the Cotton family to the Cavendishes. One of the Cavendishes had his portrait painted, and is said to have placed a curse on anyone who removed it from the house. In the 1970s, after the owner had moved out, the staircase was removed but the portrait left behind. Vandals soon broke in and took it. The house is now derelict.

Stramshall village, *c.* 1906. On the right of this view of St Michael's Road is The Hare and Hounds, where Thomas Griffin and his son of the same name were landlords from 1890 to the middle of the 1930s. Further along the road is the Primitive Methodist chapel (see p. 92), and in the distance, the parish church (see p. 89).

Stramshall Mill, *c.* 1895 (Revd Barnwell). This building was a corn mill in the eighteenth century. The waterwheel was used then to drive cotton spinning jennies for a few years before the mill reverted back to grinding corn again. The mill was always linked to a farm. In the nineteenth century Thomas Marson was the farmer and Marson & Sons were the corn millers, but at the time this picture was taken both mill and farm had been taken over by Henry Beresford. The mill probably ceased to grind corn in the early 1900s.

School and church, Hollington, 1906 (McCann). A village school for boys and girls was built at Hollington in 1837 but attracted few pupils. In the 1840s the master only taught twelve boys and the yearly expenditure of the school was no more than £13. The school shown above was built higher up the hill in 1869 and had room for over 100 pupils. In the background is the church of St John, built in 1861.

The maypole, Hollington, c. 1930. Maypole dancing on May Day could be seen in many rural schools in Staffordshire in the early nineteenth century. These children are from Hollington school. Note how the boys and girls are each divided into two equal groups by the colour of their sashes.

Lower Leigh, 1906 (McCann). On the far left is the smithy. William Emery, the blacksmith, and his men have come out to pose for the photographer. Emery also kept The Railway Inn, seen behind them, which displayed the rhyme, 'Walk in my friend and drink with me. Here's ale as good as e'er you see.' On the far right is the police station, now Chestnut Cottage.

The travelling dairy van, 1910. From the 1890s Staffordshire County Council had a horse-drawn dairy van which was parked in villages while two-week courses in butter and cheesemaking were held for farmers' wives and daughters. Until 1911 the courses were run by Miss Jenkins, whose speciality was smallholders' cheese weighing four or five pounds. This photograph was taken while the van was parked at Leigh.

The post office, Leigh, 1909 (W. Blake). At the time this picture was taken the post office was kept by John Allcocks, junior. Letters were received for delivery at 7.05 a.m. and despatched at 8.10 p.m. This is the garden at the back of the house. The entrance to the post office is on the other side. The visitor from Longton who sent this postcard wrote on it, 'Doesn't this look a restful old-world place?'

Church Leigh, 1932 (P.A. Stanier). The Star Inn, on the left, probably dates back to the eighteenth century. The licensee in 1932 was Mrs Ada Hambleton. In the distance, half hidden by trees, is the post office with the village telephone kiosk outside it. The postcard is one of a set published by Phyllis Stanier soon after she took over her mother's shop in Lower Leigh.

Leigh station, 1950. This station on the Stoke-on-Trent to Derby line was built in a Jacobean style in 1848, when the line was opened. A canopy supported by decorative iron brackets sheltered passengers travelling towards Uttoxeter. Those catching trains in the opposite direction had to cross the line by the sleepers on the level crossing and wait in the open. The station was closed to passengers in November 1966.

Park Hall, Leigh, 1908 (McCann). This house appears to have been built in the 1690s and a fireplace and panelling confirm this date. The moat, crossed by the bridge seen in the foreground, suggests that a house has existed on this site since medieval times. The gates are a magnificent work by an eighteenth-century blacksmith, but nothing is known of their origin.

WITH THE MEYNELL AT LOXLEY HALL, 2   McCANN Ph

Loxley Hall, *c.* 1910 (McCann). This is a curious house, apparently built around 1800, but with a plan and a staircase that suggest it is more than a century older. Panelling in the hall and an overmantel are from even earlier, with a date of 1607 on the frieze, but these were probably brought from another house. The Hall may have been partly rebuilt in the nineteenth century. Locally it is the centre of stories about Robin of Loxley, better known as Robin Hood. There are ballads about his adventures in the Forest of Needwood and his journey to Tutbury Fair with Clorinda, Queen of the Shepherds, who was as good with a bow as Robin himself. A horn preserved at the hall bore the initials R.H. The Sneyd-Kynnersley family, who had owned the land here since 1103, regularly acted as hosts to the Meynell Hunt.

The end of the line, 1957 (E. Talbot). The Stafford to Uttoxeter railway line was closed in 1957 and the Stephenson Locomotive Society arranged a special train for a final run on 23 March. The train stopped at every station on the line to allow passengers to take pictures. This photograph was taken during the halt at Bramshall Junction. In the centre, back to camera, is W.A. Canwell who organized the special train.

Smallwood Manor, 1960s. In 1937 the Manor was leased by Denstone College for its Preparatory Department and in 1945 money was raised to buy the Manor for the College. This postcard was produced for sales to the College's boys.

High Street, Marchington, 1902 (E. Wrench). This is the earliest postcard of Marchington, published at the beginning of the postcard craze by a Londoner called Evelyn Wrench. While on holiday in Germany at the age of seventeen, he realised how cheaply attractive postcards could be printed there. He bought photographs of towns and villages from local photographers, had them printed as postcards in Germany and sold them at a good profit. Unfortunately, his business expanded too rapidly and by 1904 he was insolvent.

The Dog and Partridge, Marchington, 1920 (McCann). The Dog and Partridge in Church Lane was built as a cottage in 1833 and only became a public house during the middle of the 1840s. Frank Sandham was the licensee in the late 1890s and he was followed by Mrs Lucy Sandham who ran the public house until the 1940s.

Marchington School, 1925. In the 1920s the school was the centre of the village with all social functions taking place there and, since there were too few adult-sized chairs, nearby householders regularly lent theirs. There were also a few 'village chairs' that were stored with whist drive tables in the Malt House opposite the school. In the 1930s the Men's Club was opened in the Malt House and social events moved there. In 1944 the school was damaged in the Fauld explosion, and in 1948 it was declared unsafe.

Houndhill, Marchington, 1910 (McCann). The Vernons had a fourteen room house here in the sixteenth century. This was largely rebuilt about 1680 so that Lord Vernon could reside here while extensive rebuilding was taking place at his main house, Sudbury Hall. It has been said that the house was sold by the Vernons after the First World War to repay gambling debts.

Woodruf's, Marchington, Nr. Uttoxeter. 15.

Woodroffe's, Marchington Woodlands, 1960 (A.W. Bourne). Bank House was owned by Thomas Coke in the sixteenth century. His son died in 1643 leaving the house to his niece 'the Widow Woodroffe'. The Woodroffes lived at Bank House for almost 200 years. The original plan and structure of the sixteenth-century house has remained largely unaltered. In 1940 Dorothy Methuen bought it, changed its name to Woodroffe's Hall and restored some of its original features. The present owners are carrying out a more thorough restoration.

Woodroffe's Hall, 1949 (Jeavons). This picture shows one of the Hall's hearths with panelling that features Tudor roses and chrysanthemums.

Four
Churches, Chapels and War Memorials

Laying the foundation stones of Dodsleigh chapel, 1908 (McCann). The foundation stones of the Primitive Methodist chapel at Dodsleigh were laid on 19 September by individuals and groups, such as Christian Endeavour, who had made donations to the building fund. One of the stones can be seen in the right foreground. The two young ladies on the right, scrambling onto a bank for a better view, are Anne Shemilt and Hannah Foster (later Mrs Davall).

Uttoxeter parish church, 1913 (W.H. Hearson). A fine parish church for Uttoxeter was built in the fourteenth century by Henry Yevele, an architect who also designed the nave of Westminster Abbey. All that remains of Yevele's church is the tower. The spire was struck by lightning in 1814, while the rest of the church was rebuilt in an imitation medieval style in 1828. This unusual view was taken from the garden of the old vicarage, visible on the right.

Interior of Uttoxeter parish church, 1904 (Valentine & Sons). The 1828 church was larger than its predecessor with room for 1,400 worshippers. The nave of six bays has north and south aisles that are separated from it by graceful arches. These arches support galleries over the aisles. The wrought iron screen at the far end of the nave was added in 1902 in memory of Prebendary Henry Abud, vicar from 1854-1902.

St Lawrence, Bramshall, 1906 (McCann). In 1830 the chancel of the parish church at Bramshall was described as being in a dangerous state, 'held together only by iron cramps which gird the outer walls'. The old church was demolished in 1835 and replaced by the present simple ashlar building, built by Thomas Fradgley of Uttoxeter at the expense of Lord Willoughby de Broke, the owner of the manor.

The bells of St Mary's, Uttoxeter, 1905 (McCann). The parish church had eight bells. Six of these were cast by Abraham Rudhall of Gloucester in the early eighteenth century and two were added in 1874 by George Kirk and the churchwardens of that time. In 1905, during repairs to the tower, it was found that the oak frame from which they hung needed replacing. This photograph from October of that year shows the bells waiting to be re-hung from a new iron frame. The man on the right is George Cope, town crier and leader of the bell-ringers. He was a woodturner by trade and made the wood from the old bell frame into an elaborate armchair with a back carved by his son Albert. In 1922, after his death, the chair was presented to the parish church.

The Japanese Fancy Fair, 1905 (McCann). In May a three day Japanese Fancy Fair and Grand Bazaar was held in Uttoxeter's Town Hall to raise £1,000 to pay for re-hanging the bells and restoring the organ of the parish church. The Hall was decorated to represent a street in Tokyo with each stall manned by helpers in Japanese costume. Richardsons, the Uttoxeter coachbuilders, even provided a rickshaw.

Queen of the May Tableau, 1905 (McCann). During the Japanese Fair, competitions such as hat trimming and soapbox making helped raise money. Entertainment was provided by 'marvellous magic shows' and a variety of children's tableaux. These solemn children posed for their Queen of the May tableau several times each day.

St Michael's, Rocester, 1907 (W.H. Hall). The parish church of St Michael in Rocester has a medieval tower that has been greatly restored. The rest of the church was rebuilt by Ewan Christian in 1872/3. An abbey of Austin Canons had been founded here in 1146 but all that remained of it by the time this picture was taken were a few humps in the field near the church, seen in the foreground.

St Peter's, Marchington, 1905 (W. Shaw). By the 1730s the parish church at Marchington had become 'rotten and ruinous'. In stormy weather 'the parishioners, terrified by the rocking and shaking of the church, run out in time of Divine Service.' By 1744 enough money had been collected to pull it down and build in its place this charming brick church with the octagonal top stage of the tower crowned by a cupola.

Marchington church, decorated for harvest thanksgiving, 1910 (McCann). To save money the new church was furnished with old items such as the box pews and three-decked pulpit were reused in the new church. In 1892, when a chancel was added to enlarge the church, a major refurbishment took place. The pulpit was cut down, and the doors were taken off the pews and used to wainscot the walls. Hinge marks can still be seen. The sixteenth-century tomb of Walter Vernon of Houndhill and his wife is on the left.

87

All Saints, Leigh, 1905 (McCann). The many burial vaults under the old church caused the floor to sink unevenly and the walls to lean from the perpendicular. The Bagots of Blithfield Hall, who owned much of the land in the parish, paid Thomas Johnson of Lichfield to rebuild it in 1846. He did so in the Decorated style, with flowing tracery in every window. The result is a Victorian gem.

Interior of All Saints, Leigh, 1905 (McCann). The church has remained largely unchanged since 1846. Note the stone rib vaulting of the chancel roof and the unusual shape of the piers. There is some fine stained glass, including the west window by Morris and Burne-Jones that is a memorial to the Revd L.F. Bagot, a nineteenth-century rector. Lighting in this picture comes from the oil lamps and candles held in brackets on the piers.

St Michael and All Angels, Stramshall, 1906 (McCann). A public subscription raised £1,200 to build this church in 1852, in preparation for Stramshall being made a separate parish. The builder was Thomas Fradgley of Uttoxeter. The vicar at this time was the Revd Charles Frederick Lowry Barnwell who served the parish from 1879 to 1932. Note the jackets and tools left by workmen tidying the approach to the church.

All Saints, Denstone, 1908 (W. Shaw). All Saints church was built in 1862 by Sir Thomas Heywood of Doveleys for the new parish of Denstone. The architect was a young G.E. Street, who also designed the vicarage, the school, the lych-gate and all the church furnishings. In the south side of the nave (visible above) each of the three windows has tracery of a different design.

Reopening the Roman Catholic church, Uttoxeter, 1914 (McCann). The first Roman Catholic church in Balance Street was consecrated in 1839. As the Leighton ironworks expanded, the Catholic community grew until a larger church was needed. In 1914 Samuel Bamford of Hawthornden Manor paid for the building to be enlarged. In this picture the procession from the presbytery, headed by the cross bearer, is about to enter the church for its official reopening in October of that year by the Archbishop of Birmingham.

Interior of the Roman Catholic church, Uttoxeter, 1920 (McCann). When the church was enlarged in 1914, two side aisles were added and a new Lady chapel was built on the south side of the chancel. Among the new furnishings were a six feet square mosaic panel of the Annunciation by Miss H. Martin and Stations of the Cross presented by Mr and Mrs Blount of Loxley Hall. A triple arch of stone and marble, rescued by Samuel Bamford from another chapel, was erected as a screen between the choir and the Lady chapel.

The Catholic chapel, Marchington (McCann). Richard Longdon, a textile manufacturer from Derby, and his sister Dorothy became Catholics in the 1930s. At Marchington Hall, where they lived, an outbuilding was converted into the small chapel shown in this photograph.

St Thomas á Becket Catholic church, Marchington, *c.* 1960 (Frith). When Richard Longdon died and Marchington Hall was sold, his sister was given permission to build a Catholic church to replace the one at the Hall. It was designed by E. Bower Norris of Stafford and opened in 1955. The small belltower on the roof was removed for safety reasons in the early 1980s when the church was renovated.

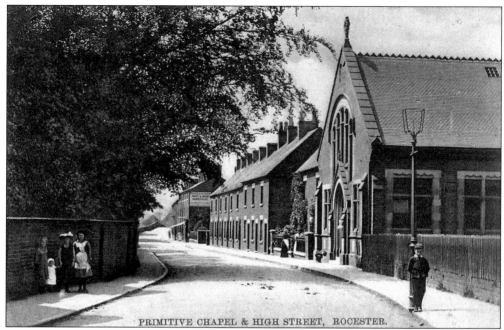

PRIMITIVE CHAPEL & HIGH STREET, ROCESTER.

Primitive Methodist chapel, Rocester, 1905 (W. Shaw). When Hugh Bourne, the founder of Primitive Methodism, visited Rocester he found it 'a very wicked place'. Two years later a small chapel was opened in High Street and in 1888 the larger chapel, seen in this picture, was built on the opposite side of the street. The chapel fell into disuse in the 1980s and in 1986 became the centre for Birmingham University's archaeological work in the village.

PRIM. METHODIST CHAPEL, STRAMSHALL.   M^cCANN P^b

The Primitive Methodist chapel, Stramshall, 1906 (McCann). The first, small Primitive Methodist chapel at Stramshall was opened in 1841 but an increase in the number of those attending led to the chapel being rebuilt in 1899.

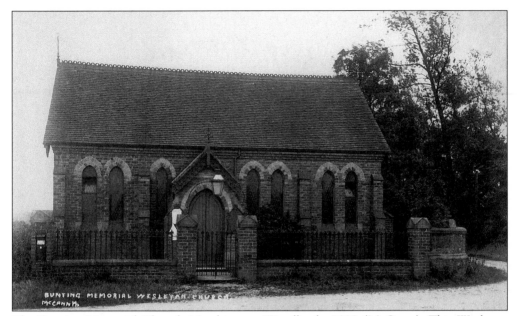

The Bunting Memorial Chapel, Marchington Woodlands, 1920 (McCann). This Wesleyan Methodist chapel was opened in the late 1870s. It took its name from Jabez Bunting (1779-1858) who had done much to organize the Wesleyan Methodist Church and complete its separation from the Anglican Church. The chapel held an anniversary service in June each year and this was always followed by tea in a marquee 'on Mr Roe's lawn'.

Dodsleigh Centenary Chapel and School, 1909. The first chapel at Dodsleigh was built by the Wesleyan Methodists in 1846, but was taken over by the Primitive Methodists. It is now the garage of a private house. A new Primitive Methodist chapel was built by Ward & Godbehere of Uttoxeter to a design by W. Campbell of Hanley in 1908-09 and is still in use as a place of worship. The laying of the foundation stones is shown on p. 81.

The Friends Meeting House, Uttoxeter, 1910 (McCann). The Society of Friends at Uttoxeter was given a house on this site in Carter Street as a meeting place in 1700. The land behind the house was used for a small burial ground. The meeting house was rebuilt around 1770 and remained substantially unchanged, except for a relocation of the doorway, until the 1960s.

Interior of the Friend's Meeting House, 1910 (McCann). The interior of the meeting house is only 25 feet by 18 feet. When this picture was taken a single iron stove, with a smokestack through the roof, was sufficient to heat it. At the west end, the raised stand seen in this postcard was flanked by benches of plank and munton. In the refurbishment of 1961/2 this was replaced by a single raised seat.

The War Memorial, Uttoxeter, 1956 (Valentine & Sons). The War Memorial, carved by Robert Bridgman & Sons of Lichfield, was unveiled on a wet Sunday in 1928 by Colonel Ratcliffe, who had commanded the 6th Battalion of the North Staffordshire Regiment in the attack on the Hohenzollern Redoubt in 1915, when many local men lost their lives.

Marchington War Memorial, 1922 (McCann). The fifteen men from Marchington who died on active service during the First World War are commemorated by this memorial over the church door. The figure represents St Michael, who led the Heavenly Hosts against the Hosts of Evil. The names of those who died in the Second World War were engraved on a processional cross, although it was not added to this memorial.

DENSTONE WAR MEMORIAL. McCANN P.

Denstone War Memorial, 1921 (McCann). The war memorial of red Hollington stone was unveiled by Major General Sir A.R. Hoskins and dedicated by the Provost of Denstone College on the evening of 13 July 1920. After the ceremony, Colonel Sir Percy Heywood, on behalf of all those who had subscribed, gave the memorial into the care of the Parish Council.

Rocester War Memorial, 1921 (McCann). On 29 October 1921 the ex-servicemen of Rocester assembled outside The Cross Keys. They marched to the parish church for a special service, before the war memorial lych-gate was unveiled by Major General Sir A.R. Hoskins, and dedicated by the Bishop of Lichfield. The town band then led the singing of 'For all the Saints'. The ceremony ended with the National Anthem and the laying of floral tributes.

War Memorial lych-gate, Rocester, 1924 (A.E. Taylor). At Rocester, public subscription paid for an oak lych-gate built on a foundation of Hollington stone, as a memorial to the nineteen local men who died in the First World War. The memorial was designed by Forshaw & Palmer of Burton-on-Trent.

Denstone College War Memorial, 1925 (McCann). This 8ft high figure of St George, holding his sword aloft by the blade as if it were a cross, was one of the College memorials to the 170 Old Boys killed in the First World War. In a ceremony in June 1925, their names were read out and 'The Last Post' sounded, before the memorial was unveiled by Col. C.P. Heywood, the grandson of the founder of the College, and dedicated by the Bishop of Lichfield.

The Memorial Chapel, Denstone College, 1920 (Marshall, Keene and Co.). The message on the back of this postcard was sent by a housemaster at the College and reads, 'This is just part of the Chapel of the College. On the left, by the hymn board, is the big Chapel. The photographs round the wall (and many more) are pictures of old College boys fallen in the War.'

Five
Days to Remember

The British Legion at Leigh, *c.* 1930 (McCann). In the years between the World Wars, Leigh had an active branch of the British Legion. This photograph shows their standard being dedicated on the lawn at the front of the Manor House, Upper Leigh. This was the home of the Bagshaws who were auctioneers in Uttoxeter. The standard bearer is Harold Heath and behind him are the standards of other Staffordshire branches of the British Legion.

Queen Victoria's Diamond Jubilee, Uttoxeter, 1897. 'A Red Letter Day in our National History' was the *Staffordshire Advertiser*'s lead-in to its description of how the Jubilee was celebrated in Uttoxeter. In the morning a procession of councillors, policemen, firemen with their horse-drawn engine *Kate*, Salvation Army, Foresters and Oddfellows with their banners, made its way to the Market Place. There, everyone joined in the National Anthem. In the afternoon over 1,000 children marched in procession from the Market Place to a field near Oldfields Hall for sports and tea. Each child was presented with a Jubilee Cup by Mr Bunting and a Jubilee Medal by Mr Bamford. In the evening a torch-lit procession of cyclists in grotesque costumes rode to a bonfire. Dancing went on in High Street until the early hours of the next morning.

Edward VII passing through Uttoxeter, 1907 (McCann). When Edward VII visited Staffordshire in November 1907 he stayed with Lord Shrewsbury at Ingestre Hall and also visited Lord Shrewsbury's other house – Alton Towers. On 21 November he returned from Alton Towers via Uttoxeter. The pilot car, belonging to Lord Shrewsbury, made sure the way was clear and that the King's chauffeur did not lose his way.

The King's car, Uttoxeter, 1907 (McCann). On the outskirts of Uttoxeter the King's car had a puncture. After a delay the King proceeded in another car supplied by Lord Shrewsbury. Here the King is being driven along a lavishly decorated High Street.

Oddfellows' procession, Rocester, *c.* 1910 (McCann). The Houldsworth Lodge of Oddfellows took its name from the owners of the cotton mill at Rocester in the middle of the nineteenth century. Their clubhouse was a room at The Cross Keys and their anniversary procession was held on Whit Monday. This photograph shows members, including members of the juvenile lodge, assembling outside The Cross Keys.

Oddfellows procession, Rocester, *c.* 1910 (McCann). The procession, led by a band, marched from The Cross Keys to the parish church for a special anniversary service, paraded around the village and then returned to their club room for a dinner. In this photograph the procession is passing Dwyer's grocery store in Ashbourne Road. Dwyer himself has come out on the pavement to watch the Oddfellows go by.

The Flower Show, Leigh, 1905. The annual Flower Show was first held in 1883. By the early 1900s it was attracting visitors from a wide area, with special 'Flower Show' fares on the North Staffordshire Railway. Besides competitive classes including flowers, fruit, vegetables, bread, cheese and butter, there were also Punch and Judy performances, pierrot shows, and swings and roundabouts. In this photograph Mr and Mrs Johnson of Tean are talking to Mrs Mary Nutt and Mrs Edmund Sims.

The King's Memorial Service, Uttoxeter, 1910 (McCann). A combined service to mark the death of Edward VII was held in the parish church on 20 May 1910. The service was led by the vicar, Revd W.C. Granville Sharp, and the lessons read by Revd W. Taggart (Wesleyan) and Revd H.A. Evans (Congregational). The clergy, followed by members of the Urban and Rural District Councils, are seen in the Market Place after leaving the church at the end of the service.

Coronation Day at Uttoxeter, 1911 (McCann). The Coronation of King George V and Queen Mary on 22 June was celebrated enthusiastically in Uttoxeter. At 8.00 a.m. the Territorials assembled in the Market Place to fire a noisy *joie-de-feu* in the air before the Ironworks Band played the National Anthem. At 10.30 a.m. a procession formed in the Smithfield and marched to services at the parish church and St Mary's Catholic Church. These photographs show the procession in High Street (above) and the scene in the Market Place just after it had passed (below).

Coronation Day tree planting in Uttoxeter, 1911 (McCann). After the church services, the procession reformed and made its way to Park Place where an oak tree was planted by Mr A.C. Bunting, Chairman of the Urban District Council. In this photograph, taken shortly after the ceremony, the tree can be seen in the background to the right of the signpost. Beyond it, Mr Bunting's carriage is waiting to take him back to the Town Hall.

Coronation bonfire, Uttoxeter, 1911 (McCann). On the afternoon of Coronation Day a gala was held at the racecourse. Children were presented with a coronation mug and medal before a tea. In the evening a bonfire, built by the scouts, was lit as one of a chain across England. Signal rockets, set off from high places, made sure all bonfires were lit at exactly 10.00 p.m. Each one sent up a bouquet of rockets at 11.00 p.m., followed by a mass singing of the National Anthem.

Henry Bamford's coming of age, 1912 (McCann). Henry John Bamford, only son of John Bamford of Oldfields Hall, was twenty-one on 2 January 1912. At 4.00 a.m. on that day, a fire was lit on Hockley Meadow to roast a bullock polled across two trestles. By 12.30 p.m. the carcass was cooked. Henry Bamford himself cut the first slice and then 200 more slices were cut and given away. The church bells rang, and the workers at the Leighton Ironworks struck a twenty-one anvil salute at noon.

Henry Bamford's coming of age dinner, 1912 (McCann). In the evening, the largest room in the Leighton Ironworks had been cleared and laid out for a dinner in honour of Henry Bamford. Banners with the words 'Welcome' and 'Long Life and Happiness' were hung at either end of the room and twenty special Kitson lamps were brought in to light it. The 800 guests included employees, friends and members of public bodies.

Peace Day, Uttoxeter, 1919 (McCann). Although the armistice of 11 November 1918 ended the fighting in the First World War, a peace treaty was not signed until 28 June 1919. The government declared that 19 July 1919 should be celebrated as Peace Day. At Uttoxeter a procession of soldiers, sailors, ex-servicemen, nurses, scouts and members of the Workers' Union, led by Bamford's band, paraded from the Town Hall through streets decorated with flags, to the racecourse. At the racecourse sports were held and a cricket match was played. A public dinner for ex-servicemen was held at the Town Hall and a tea for the children at the racecourse. The day ended with a bonfire at Highfields.

Presentation to the National Railway Queen, 1935 (McCann). In June 1935 Ruby Dovey, daughter of a London engine driver and National Railway Queen, was invited to Uttoxeter. After arriving by train, she toured Elkes' factory, where she was presented with this Silver Jubilee tin of biscuits. Her attendants were Enid Ottewell, Margaret Russell, Sheila Hassall, Betty Walker, all children of local railwaymen. In the evening she crowned Kathleen Jardine of Stubwood as Uttoxeter Carnival Queen and attended the Carnival Ball.

Opening the new Catholic school, Uttoxeter, 1930 (McCann). A Catholic school had been opened in Balance Street in 1871, but by the 1920s it was overcrowded. The foundation stone of a new school at Mount Pleasant was laid by Samuel Bamford in September 1929 and the new building was opened by His Grace the Archbishop of Birmingham in April 1930.

The Meynell Hunt, Smallwood Manor, 1907 (McCann). Smallwood Manor was built early in the nineteenth century. In the 1850s it was the home of Thomas Webb, who owned a glass works at Tutbury. In the 1880s he sold the house to Mr Hodgson who pulled it down and built the one seen here in its place. The design is said to reflect his wife's wish that the house should remind her of Eastbourne, where she spent many happy holidays.

The Meynell Hunt, Uttoxeter, 1937 (McCann). In 1937 the Hunt revived the Boxing Day meet at Uttoxeter Market Place. A record crowd turned out for 'the charming and picturesque spectacle' and a collection was taken in aid of the Uttoxeter Nursing Fund. The Hunt moved off at 11.00 a.m. under joint masters, Capt. M.J. Kingscote (on the white horse) and Capt. R.W. Verelst, to try the coverts at Eaton Woods.

'Salute the Soldier' parade, Uttoxeter, 1944 (McCann). The target for the town's 'Salute the Soldier' week in May was £250,000 for the war effort. The week began with this parade. Its 1,800 personnel and 7 bands made it the largest precession ever seen in the town. In this picture, sailors and WRNS are passing the saluting base. The purpose of the racing pigeons in their wicker baskets on the right is uncertain. Later in the week, other events helped to raise the sum invested in savings to a record £336,979.

Victory party, Westlands Road, Uttoxeter, 1945. This is one of two Victory parties organized by those living in Westlands Road on 26 May. Police allowed the road to be closed, mothers shared rations to provide food and children were sent off to the cinema matinee while tables were laid in the street. Each child also received an orange, a threepenny bit and a bag of sweets and biscuits. The boy holding the Victory shield is Tony Taylor.

Coronation decorations, Uttoxeter, 1953 (McCann). Street decorations were a feature of the 1953 Coronation celebrations everywhere. Those in London attracted hordes of visitors. The Uttoxeter C of E school took all of its pupils to the capital by train and toured the streets by bus, before visiting London Zoo. In Uttoxeter, the council set an example to local shopkeepers. In the photograph above, the Town Hall is being decorated and, below, the Kiosk is covered in greenery surmounted by a crown.

Coronation Party, Uttoxeter, 1953 (McCann). The Coronation was marked by a number of parties. The Council arranged one for mothers with children below school age. There were also street parties, though some of these were driven indoors by rain. School children had parties and were presented with Coronation mugs. In this picture the Chairman of the UDC, Councillor A.O. Davies, is seen with all the helpers before one of the indoor parties.

Elite Cinema, 1953 (McCann). The Elite Cinema was photographed during the week beginning 15 June when it was showing the full length Technicolor film of the Coronation of Elizabeth II, titled, *A Queen is Crowned*.

Six

The Working Life

Corset makers, Uttoxeter, early 1900s. Richard Cooper was manufacturing corsets and stays at Ashbourne in the 1850s. In 1890 he expanded his business into the old canal warehouse at The Wharf, where this photograph was taken. Richard Cooper later took as his partner G.E. Gather. In January 1921 Gather gave a tea in the Town Hall for all the workers to mark the coming of age of his son, George, who had also joined the business.

Ploughing, Rocester, 1944 (McCann). The district around Uttoxeter has always been a farming area and it is appropriate that a number of photographs at the start of this section contain aspects of rural life. In this picture Arthur Salt of Rocester is seen competing in the tractor ploughing section of a ploughing and hedge laying competition, organized by the Rocester War Charities Committee, in aid of Red Cross parcels for prisoners of war. Mr Salt was second in his class.

Hedge laying, Loxley, 1928 (McCann). This is an earlier competition where G.W. Swinson of Leigh is posing with his felling axe after laying his section of hedge. The judges are standing in the background.

Timber hauling, Hollington, 1910. Trees were still felled and trimmed using axes and handsaws when this picture was taken. The trunks were lifted onto a dray using a simply rigged pulley. Four heavy horses could haul away an impressive weight.

The Uttoxeter creamery, 1928. In 1897 a creamery was built on Brookside Road, which at this time was a muddy track to the Town Meadows. It expanded rapidly and, at one time, thirteen million gallons of milk a year were being turned into butter, cheese and condensed milk. The name of the company changed several times (in 1928 it was Wiltshire United Dairies) before it became part of Unigate. These lorries were used to collect milk from farms around Uttoxeter.

Horse fair, Balance Street, Uttoxeter (McCann). Animals have been sold in Uttoxeter street markets since the Middle Ages. Different animals were traditionally sold in different places. Between the end of Balance Street and the Market Place, for example, was the sheep market with temporary pens made from hurdles. In the nineteenth century all these markets moved to Smithfield, except for this horse fair held in Balance Street every September.

Uttoxeter Smithfield. When the Town Hall was built in 1854, a Smithfield livestock market was opened in the space behind it and the long established fortnightly cattle sales moved there. The Smithfield and its tolls belonged to the Lord of the Manor until July 1897, when a referendum of inhabitants voted 604 to 56 for the Town Council to purchase them. Major improvements and extensions took place in 1912 and 1934/5, leading to a larger market area and more covered space. These two photographs show the Smithfield in 1921, photographed by Alfred McCann for a town guide (above), and on 14 September 1945, by Gerald McCann (below).

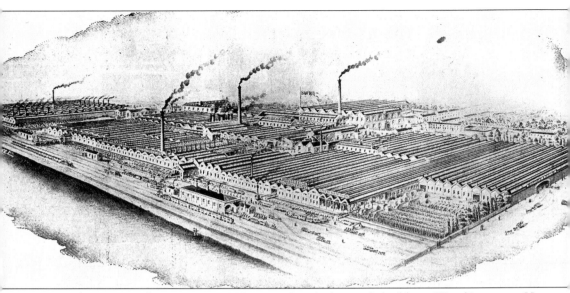

Leighton Ironworks, Uttoxeter, 1907. Henry Bamford, son of a builder at Wood Lane near Hoar Cross, set himself up as an ironmonger in the Market Place, Uttoxeter, in 1845. His son, Samuel, started a small foundry at the old canal wharf to make castings for the business. In 1871 the foundry moved to this larger site at Leighton in Uttoxeter and expanded to make a range of agricultural implements. When this bird's-eye view was taken, the factory covered twenty-two acres.

Leighton Ironworks, 1940s (McCann). After 1907 the works expanded steadily. This photograph is one of a series that McCann took showing workers and machines at the ironworks. Note the large overhead extractor to remove dust generated by the machine.

Advertisement for H. Bamford & Sons, in *The Ironmonger*, January 1891. The number of gold medals awarded at agricultural trials shows the outstanding quality of the machines produced by the company.

The first JCB factory. John Cyril Bamford rented this workshop on Derby Road, Uttoxeter, in 1945 to make farm trailers out of army surplus materials and scrap. Wartime restrictions were responsible for there being no electricity supply and so everything was literally hand built. The first trailer built here is now on display at the Rocester works. After eighteen months he moved to outbuildings at Crakemarsh Hall because his landlady objected to Sunday working.

JCB, the first Rocester factory, 1950. Late in 1950 J.C. Bamford moved from Crakemarsh Hall to these buildings at Rocester. The building with a tiled roof in the centre of the picture was a disused cheese factory once operated by Wiltshire United Dairies. The building with a curved roof was a Dutch hay barn built in 1946 in an unsuccessful attempt to establish a cattle sale yard. The round concrete blocks are wartime tank traps from the White Bridge. The modern day factory developed from this beginning.

Bunting's Brewery, Uttoxeter, 1911. The Uttoxeter Brewery Company was formed in 1829 by Thomas Earp, a brewer, and Edward Saunders, a maltster. By the 1870s it was run by Keates and Wood, and in the 1890s it was bought by Charles Bunting. Bunting was already the licensee of The Cross Keys, a wine spirit and porter merchant, and the leaser of the refreshment room at the station. The brewery was sold to Parker's (Burslem) Brewery in February 1929 and closed in the 1930s.

Bunting's delivery drays, 1910. The drays were backed up to a platform of the same height as the floor of the dray so that the barrels could be rolled on and off without lifting. These horse-drawn drays were a familiar sight in the main streets of Uttoxeter.

Richardson & Son, Uttoxeter, 1907. George Richardson, a wheelwright in Bradley Street, moved into these premises on the corner of Park Street in the 1840s and expanded his business to make a variety of horse-drawn coaches and carriages. By 1907 the business was beginning to change again. Repairing motor vehicles and selling bicycles were added to the traditional coachbuilding. By the time George's great-grandson sold the business in 1962 it had become a motor garage.

Richardson's workers, c. 1910. Coachbuilding needed men with a variety of skills for working with wood, metal and leather (for upholstery). In this photograph many of the workmen are carrying a tool to indicate their particular skill. The man on the left is said to be William Richardson.

A gig, 1900 (McCann). Gigs were popular with doctors and other professional men because they looked smart, yet were light and easily pulled by one horse. Different kinds of wood were used for different parts – including ash for the frame, oak for the spokes and mahogany for the panels. At least ten coats of paint were laid on the side panels and each one was rubbed down. These coats of paint were followed by six or eight coats of varnish to provide a good finish.

Putting an iron tyre on a wheel, 1950s (McCann). Richardsons retained traditional skills into the 1950s. Here an iron tyre is being heated before being hammered over the wheel on the left. As the tyre cooled, it contracted and clenched the fellies of the rim tightly over the spokes.

Elkes' hand cart, Uttoxeter, c. 1930 (McCann). Charles Elkes opened his bakery, confectionery shop and dining room on the corner of Carter Street around 1906. When he died, his business was carried on by his son, Wilfred, who had this loaf-shaped handcart made by Richardsons as a trade entry in the carnival procession. It was later used to deliver bread and cakes around the town.

Dove Valley Bakeries, Uttoxeter, 1958 (Elkes). Charles Elkes started making biscuits in the bakery behind his shop on the corner of Carter Street in 1924. In 1927 he started Dove Valley Bakeries on Cheadle Road to produce biscuits and cakes on a larger scale. The bakeries expanded rapidly and became C.H. Elkes & Sons when Wilfred and Samuel Elkes joined the business. This postcard view of the factory was published by the company and used to acknowledge orders.

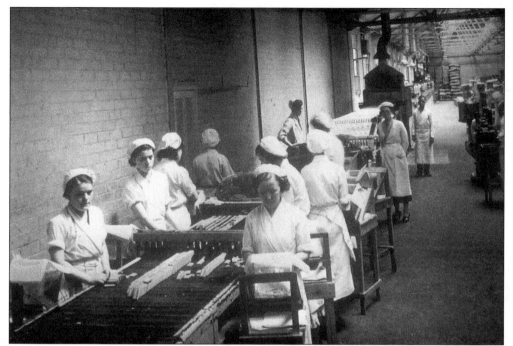

Biscuit packing, 1940s. This photograph shows biscuits being packed at the Dove Valley Bakeries soon after the Second World War. The biscuits appear to be the company's popular malted milk brand, marketed with the slogan, 'Next time you see a pair of cows peering at you from a biscuit, they're probably Elkes.'

Elkes Girl Pipers, 1936/7 (Elkes). In the autumn of 1934 at C.H. Elkes and Sons, Pipe Major W.E. Macmillan formed this troupe known as The Dove Valley Girls or Elkes Girl Pipers. Their Highland dress, bagpipes and drums soon became a popular attraction at local fêtes. They are photographed here outside Hawthornden Manor, Uttoxeter.

Rocester cotton mill, 1907 (W.H. Hall). The water-driven corn mill on this site was bought by Richard Arkwright in 1781, and rebuilt with two (later three) waterwheels providing power for carding and spinning cotton. The mill employed 200 people and cottages had to be built to house them. In 1805 Arkwright sold out to Richard Briddon. In 1830 the mill was bought by Thomas Houldsworth, a Lancashire spinner, who encouraged schooling for the children of both the workers and the villagers. In 1874 the mill was sold to Walter and Charles Lyons of Tutbury Mill Co. who replaced the water wheels with water turbines. In 1907 the owners were the Fine Cotton Spinners & Doubling Association, with Sir William Houldsworth as Chairman. This photograph shows boys and young women, who made up the bulk of the workers, and a few older men leaving the mill at 1.00 p.m. for their lunch break.

The Tutbury Mill Co. Ltd., Rocester, Staffs.

Rocester cotton mill. In this aerial view Millholme, 'a genteel family home' for the mill owner, is on the left. The four-storey block added by the Tutbury Mill Co. in the 1870s is in the centre with the older buildings to the right of it. The mill pond was on the right until the weir collapsed in 1943 and the mill had to be converted to electric power. Its life as a spinning mill ended in 1990 when the building was bought by JCB Excavators Ltd.

Mill Lane, Rocester, 1908 (H.P. Hansen). Mill workers are shown leaving the cotton mill and in the right foreground schoolchildren are watching the photographer.

Workers at Hollington stone quarry, 1910. The sandstone quarries at Hollington were not worked on a large scale until the early nineteenth century. The excellent red and white freestone became well known and was used extensively for repairing old churches and building new ones. It is still one of the best types of stone and was chosen when Coventry Cathedral had to be rebuilt after being bombed.

Red Hill Bank brickworks, Rocester, 1902 (E. Wrench). Red Hill Bank brick and tileworks were probably started by Joseph Hordern around 1850 to take advantage of transport by the newly opened railway line. In the 1890s they were leased to Arthur Hewins who tried to expand his business by leasing Hazelstrine Quarry near Stafford. He failed to pay for machinery that he had taken over with the quarry and was declared bankrupt in January 1907. The site is now part of the J.C. Bamford Excavators' factory.